THE INDUSTRIAL REVOLUTION

Britain, 1770–1810

Jonathan Downs

D0169469

SHIRE LIVING HISTORIES

How we worked • How we played • How we lived

First published in Great Britain in 2010 by Shire
Publications Ltd, Midland House, West Way, Botley,
Oxford OX2 0PH, United Kingdom.
44-02 23rd Street, Suite 219, Long Island City, NY11101,
USA.

E-mail: shire@shirebooks.co.uk www.shirebooks.co.uk

A CIP catalogue record for this book is available from the
British Library.

Shire Living Histories no. 4 • ISBN-13: 978 0 74780 781 0

Jonathan Downs has asserted his right under the
Copyright, Designs and Patents Act, 1988, to be identified
as the author of this book.

Designed by Myriam Bell Design, France and typeset in
Perpetua, Jenson Text and Gill Sans.
Printed in China through Worldprint Ltd.

10 11 12 13 14   10 9 8 7 6 5 4 3 2 1

COVER IMAGE
The Forge, by James Sharples (c. 1751–1811). Iron was the
driving force behind the Industrial Revolution.

ACKNOWLEDGEMENTS

Jonathan Downs would like to thank the General Editor
Peter Furtado, Joe Moran of Cowan's Auctions in
Cincinnati, Bill Harriman of the BASC, Ian Hamilton,
Maryanne Willson LL.M., and Alison Dalby of the
National Trust for their generous assistance and support.

Illustrations are acknowledged as follows:

Ancient Art and Architecture, page 9 (bottom); Blackburn
Museum and Art Gallery/The Bridgeman Art Library,
cover image; The Bridgeman Art Library, pages 25, 35, 44,
48, and 55 (top); British Library, pages 11, 13 (top), 20,
23, 26, 34 (bottom), 47, 52–3, 76, 77, and 80; Cowan
Auctions, Cincinnati, page 57; Sarah-Jane Downing,
page 73; English Heritage Photo Library, page 72;
Flickr: Steve Brown, page 7, N. B. Perch, Page 8,
Piedmont Fossil, page 10, Brian Mossemenear, page 16,
Andy Marsh, page 22; Giraudon/The Bridgeman Art
Library, pages 36, 39 (bottom), 40 (top), and 75; Mary
Evans Picture Library, pages 4, 12, 17, 19, 22 (top), 28,
33, 34 (top), 49 (bottom), 50, 54 (bottom), 62, 64, 65,
66, 68, 70, 74 (top), 81, 82, and 83; National Portrait
Gallery/Bridgeman Art Library, page 15 (top);
New College, Oxford/The Bridgeman Art Library,
page 14 (bottom); Robert Opie Collection, pages 18, 38,
39 (top), 41 (bottom), 46 (top and bottom), 40 (top), 54
(top), 60, 61 67, 84, and 85; Royal College of Surgeons/
The Bridgeman Art Library, page 78; Eve Saint Simmons
(iknow-uk), page 15 (bottom); Science Museum,
London/The Bridgeman Art Library, pages 7, 9 (bottom),
and 31; Scottish National Portrait Gallery/The Bridgeman
Art Library, page 9 (top); Shire Publishing – Chris
Holland, pages 42–3, and Pete Crooks, pages 58–9;
Yale Center for British Art/The Bridgeman Art Library,
pages 40 and 55 (bottom).

All other pictures are the copyright of the author.

Shire Publications is supporting the Woodland Trust, the UK's leading woodland conservation charity, by funding the dedication of trees.

CONTENTS

PREFACE

WE ALL CARRY IMAGES with us of life in the Industrial Revolution: starving workers in dangerous factories, overseen by hard-eyed managers until they return to their filthy hovels on the brink of exhaustion, while their neighbours, the hand-loom weavers and others disempowered by the new technology, go round smashing the machinery that has stolen their livelihood.

While there is much truth in these images, some of them derive from the mid-nineteenth century when the worst abuses were described (not least by Charles Dickens, hence their ability to sear themselves on our imaginations) and eventually tackled. In this volume we look at the earlier generation of industrialism, a time that saw invention and innovation in mechanisation and in power. It certainly set the pattern for what was to come, with streets, neighbourhoods and even whole towns of slums thrown up to serve the new factories, and workers treated as inhuman sources of labour, who could resort to few rights either legal or traditional. Yet the new world offered genuine opportunities for some, and gave others a route out of the dead end of a countryside where other changes had drastically reduced the opportunities for work.

For this period we concentrate, naturally, on the strange new life endured by these workers. But others enjoyed a new prosperity, and their experience was as much part of British history as that of the new working classes. In this volume, Jonathan Downs paints a rounded picture of life in a society on the brink of dramatic and permanent change.

Peter Furtado
General Editor

Opposite:
The elegant
Bridge Street,
Chester,
c. 1780.

INTRODUCTION

THE TERM 'INDUSTRIAL REVOLUTION' is somewhat misleading; we could be forgiven for thinking that, one day some time in the eighteenth century, Britain descended from a peaceful rural idyll and awoke to an infernal, smoke-blackened urban squalor the next. The expression itself was coined only in hindsight of decades, or indeed centuries, of change. Although similar developments also occurred in other nations, Britain was the engine behind this global 'revolution' – experiencing deep social and economic change which shaped a kingdom, gave rise to an empire and, consequently, created the modern industrialised world.

Today historians see that the smouldering fuse which was to lead to this explosion of development had been lit as far back as the Middle Ages. The ongoing revolution gathered pace in the early decades of the 1700s and reached deep into the Victorian era – and in a way it continues to this day, as we too live in a world of constant technological innovation. Britain would see some of its greatest changes after 1770, engineered by a natural entrepreneurial spirit and an extraordinary pool of inventive genius which continued to grow with each new development.

In 1776, the same year as the old order of Georgian rule in America was shattered by the Declaration of Independence, James Watt (1736–1819), a Scots mathematician and engineer, put into operation the first effective steam engine of the modern world capable of driving machinery. Previously, the only sources of power available to industry had been wind, water, animal and human – the arrival of Watt's fuel-efficient 'energy on tap' had much the same impact upon eighteenth-century industry as the computer has had on business today. However, Watt by no means invented the steam engine – it had been in use since the late seventeenth century, employed in pumping water from mines. But these earlier devices were very inefficient, losing almost 80 per cent of their energy in the process.

Opposite: Arkwright's cotton mills, painted in the 1790s by Joseph Wright of Derby.

The great bridge at Ironbridge, spanning the River Severn, the first of its kind in the world, completed in 1779.

Thomas Newcomen's great engine of 1712 required large amounts of coal to run; and in areas like Cornwall where coal was scarce, it was very expensive to operate. It was Watt who found a solution, radically redesigning the engine to use higher pressure and burn 75 per cent less fuel. Its first application was in mining operations in 1776 in the Midlands, Shropshire, and east London. Mine-owners recognised its value at once and orders began to pour in. Working with his business partner Matthew Boulton (1728–1809), Watt further devised driving pistons with smooth rotational motions which allowed for grinding, milling and weaving processes to be powered by steam as well. Soon the factories rising across the landscape would have, at their heart, Watt's new powerhouse.

Although this development by Watt and subsequent work by Murdoch, Hornblower, Trevithick and others, created a new mechanised platform for industry, a separate revolution in agriculture was needed to support the application of these technological wonders. In the mid-eighteenth century farming became more industrially efficient as a number of owners acquired larger areas of land which they enclosed to allow them to farm as they wished. Food production increased dramatically and supported a growing population. One might imagine that new farming technology, such as Meikle's threshing machine of 1786, edged farm labourers into unemployment, but in fact the number of agricultural labourers stayed about the same in this period – the real problem was that there was not enough work for the ever-increasing numbers of available farmhands and unskilled labourers. It is estimated that the population of England alone rose from 5.5 million in 1700 to some 9 million in 1801. The majority of them lived on the land, but there was simply not enough work to match their numbers.

Thousands were forced to leave lands traditionally inhabited by their forebears, their rights to graze their meagre flocks or fowl, or to forage for fodder or fuel, now lost forever. The landed gentry sought to acquire as much land as possible, often with the support of smaller landholders who sold their own parcels and set up in new enterprises elsewhere. The newly purchased arable land was then enclosed by the hedges and stone walls which have since become hallmarks of the British

countryside, but which then spelt ruin and despair for many. These enclosed lands were much more manageable and ideal for industrial-level food production; they attracted higher rents and ended the medieval village-based system of farming in large open fields. Unskilled workers were now cut off from their ancient sources of income. As common lands dwindled in size, in some cases leaving only scraps of uncultivatable land, such as rocky hillsides, many subsistence farmers were plunged further into poverty. Although land had been

James Watt, engineer and designer of the two-chamber steam engine; after the portrait by William Beechey.

A replica of the spinning mule frame invented by Samuel Crompton, c. 1772–79.

9

enclosed since the Middle Ages, especially under the Tudors, from 1750 numerous regional 'Inclosure Acts' sealed the fate of many families. Unskilled men, women, and children were driven to the cities and towns, drawn by the only other places where their labour was in high demand: the new factories and foundries. Herein lies the key to the industrial revolution in Britain: there was a vast number of workers ready to stoke the furnaces of the brave new world. Their hands, as much as Watt's steam engine, powered the development of the modern age.

The landmarks of this new era were the 'manufactories', designed in the new architecture of industry, built in the towns or on the riversides; around them sprang streets of terraced houses. Our understanding of this is coloured by nineteenth-century images of wretched workers enslaved in their 'dark satanic mills'. It is true that conditions were very poor in most cases, but this was not entirely the fault of industry. Working conditions had always been harsh for the labourer, but it was not until overworked manpower was concentrated in factories belching smoke from their obtrusive, alien chimneys, that the educated classes finally took notice. In fact, some factories were almost pleasant, situated in the grounds of the local manor-house, among gardens and pasture, the workers' brick cottages only a short walk away – a vast improvement on the hovels occupied by many unskilled agricultural labourers engaged in a back-breaking dawn-till-dusk working life.

A jasperware Wedgwood vase, c. 1785, a fine example of British craftsmanship. The neoclassical themes of such objects had become popular after the discovery of Herculaneum in 1738 and Pompeii in 1748.

Of all the industries, textile production was the one that took the most direct role in shaping the urban landscape, employing hundreds of thousands. British broadcloth had long been the envy of Europe, its export the cornerstone of the national economy, accounting for roughly a quarter of Britain's trade. The industry, though, was limited by its structure: wool was spun and woven by hand in weavers' cottages, their produce taken by horse and cart or river barge, towed along the as-yet undeveloped waterways. With expanding markets and raw materials aplenty, the textile industry – which now included cotton weaving as well – was ready to boom. Technical innovations abounded by mid-century: one of the first factory mills was created in Birmingham as early as 1742 – but its power source was nothing more than the donkey, and the venture soon failed; however, the second attempt in Northampton operated for over twenty years. Industrialist Richard Arkwright (1732–92) and designer Samuel Crompton (1753–1827) brought developments to spinning technology and opened factory mills in Lancashire to house the new machines.

Patented in 1770, and possibly the second-most famous invention of the time, the spinning jenny increased the production of a spinner nearly tenfold. The first machine of inventor James Hargreaves (1720–78) could spin eleven threads at once, but in 1783 it was noted by the Society for the Encouragement of the Arts, Manufactures and Commerce, 'The construction of this kind of

machine, called a *Spinning jenny*, has since been much improved, and is now at so high a degree of perfection, that one woman is thereby enabled with ease to spin a hundred threads of cotton at a time.' Arkwright used water-wheels to power his multiple spinning machines, but in the following decades the textile industry was transformed again by the impact of the Boulton & Watt steam engine.

The *Essex* East Indiaman, refitted at anchor in Bombay Harbour. It was such vessels that brought Britain its steady supply of exotic materials from the subcontinent. Aquatint, 1785.

The transport of the produce of these new factories was not restricted to old-fashioned horse and cart. A canal system was developed to keep pace with the demands of the new towns and cities, connecting the mill towns of the north not only to Liverpool but to marketplaces as far afield as Bristol and London. The road network was improved, as observers were quick to complain of town streets cut by deep ruts of cartwheels, 'running with filth and ordure'. Economics drove the country towards efficiency and productivity. Invention continued: with the construction of the canal system and road network, it was not long before the application of Watt's steam engine to the matter of transport. Although the railways are most associated with the Victorians, it was in the early years of the nineteenth century that the first experiments were conducted, by men such as Richard Trevithick and George Stephenson.

As mills, foundries and factories sprang up, whole streets, towns and populations sprawled around them to create the great hive of industry which Britain had become. As to the people, a once largely agricultural society adapted to new surroundings, new dangers and diseases, their calloused hands now battered by a different toil. By 1820, at the end of King George III's long reign, the face of Britain had changed forever. So too, would she change the world.

FAMILY LIFE

THE BEGINNING and end of the working day in the industrial Georgian era are difficult to pinpoint precisely; one plantation worker in the Caribbean recalled he slaved from 'can see to can't see', and this was the general rule of thumb for labourers in Britain as well. The advent of the factory clock changed this. Often sounding its bells at 5.45 a.m., it started the factory worker's day as early as a domestic servant might. No one could argue with the factory clock, which ruled the life of its workers. It eventually became apparent that such clocks were often set to strike earlier than the official hour to gather the workforce, and to run slowly during the day in order to keep them at their machines for longer. William Murdoch (1754–1839), an innovator after Watt, established a means of lighting factories by gas lamp so that work could continue long after dark.

Of all the members of the working-class household it must be the matriarch who suffered the most. As well as being forced to work in the factories or on the land with the men – unless edged out as second-class labour in favour of men and machines – she was duty-bound to provide domestic service as well, work which would have been easily as arduous as a shift at the mechanical power-loom yet which went unrecognised. William Hutton, once a child labourer in a Derby silk-mill and later the first historian of Birmingham, wrote with some feeling of his mother's devotion to the family in the 1720s: 'My poor mother more than once, one infant on her knee, and a few more hanging about her, have all fasted a whole day; and when food arrived, she has suffered them, with a tear, to take *her* share. Time produced nothing but rags and children.'

The man of the house, however, bore the legal responsibility for the family upon his shoulders alone, and their condition, be it prosperous or poor, was judged to be his personal success or failure. The legalities of marriage were arguably more far-reaching than those of today; common-law vows, whereby a man promised to take a

Opposite:
The vicar of the parish receiving tithes from a woman and a small boy, 1793.

13

The condition of Britain and Europe: a comment on the state of Great Britain and the continent in 1803–04. John Bull is sitting under an oak tree supported by 'Trade and commerce'. Napoleon is represented as a dragon figure; the three lions represent the British armed forces.

woman 'to wife', if said in front of witnesses, was just as binding as that of a full-scale church wedding. Much as any legal contract, if a token of any monetary value, such as a gold ring or even less, were also exchanged, then the contract was irrevocable. A parish church wedding required three weeks of banns to be read, but there were several 'shortcut' churches – the one at St Pancras was so popular it was said 'they stand behind one another' as if ready for a country dance. With the rise of the industrialist and the shifting of class boundaries, a marriage to a man of means was considered the ideal, as expressed with more than a little irony in the opening line of Jane Austen's *Pride and Prejudice* (1813): 'It is a truth universally acknowledged, that a single man in possession of a good fortune, must be in want of a wife.' Although sons were more useful to a household as working money-earners, a daughter could theoretically catch the eye of a captain of industry, thus raising the family to greater social status, or at least monetary security.

La promenade en famille, or a sketch from life, by James Gillray, 1797, shows King George III being driven to distraction by his children. The opposite was probably more true.

Georgian morals are often contrasted to Victorian, the former era traditionally considered bawdy and loose, the latter tight-lipped and repressed. 'Respectability' however, had its origins in the Georgian industrial period – in the 1780s men and women would watch one's speech in genteel society, and consider their standing and character as never before. This was doubtless the influence of family upbringing, a popular religious revival and an increased religious diversity in society. Puritans, Evangelists, Calvinists, Wesley's Arminian Methodists and general Dissenters or 'Rational Dissenters' – all had complaints about the laxness of the regular clergy.

Being a Dissenter involved wearing a metaphorical social badge. William Hutton had this to say:

> My ancestors have been steady in religion, for they were Dissenters from the first establishment of that sect under Bishop Hooper. They have been as steady in their love of peace, and of pudding; remarkable for memory; not much given to receive, keep, or pay money; often sensible, always modest. The males inactive, the females distinguished for capacity.

John Wesley (1703–91) preacher and founder of Arminianism and the later Methodist movement, portrayed here in 1788.

Religious choices reached into the workplace which, even if officially bound to the Church of England, could show tolerance and leniency:

> We were the only family of Dissenters connected with the Silk-mill. One of the clerks wished to make me a convert to the established

'A La Ronde', a unique 16-sided house built in Exmouth by cousins Jane and Mary Parminter, on their return in 1795 from a ten-year Grand Tour of Europe. Now a National Trust property, it contains many mementoes of their travels including a feather frieze and a shell-encrusted gallery.

The Methodist Church in the centre of Welton, Lincolnshire. These were often humble structures by comparison to those of the traditional clergy. Before the amalgamation of the various groups there were chapels in Welton for the Wesleyan Methodists, the Free Church, the Primitive Methodists and the Reform Methodists.

church, and threw out the lure of a halfpenny every Sunday if I should attend divine service there. This purchased me; and my father, who was a moderate man, winked at the purchase. This proves an assertion of Sir Robert Walpole, "That every man has his price." None could be much lower than mine.

The rise of religious dissent is not surprising considering the poor management of the nation's spiritual health by the established Church of England. Parsons were allotted their parishes and these became their source of income – they would rely on their flock to provide a decent living, often through the land owned by the parish and let to local farmers or workers. Some performed very little for their reward – many did not live in their parish; it became such a problem that a law was passed in 1808 to see that they did. If a rector read the service on a Sunday, and visited the sick when sent for, wrote commentator George Pryme (1781–1868), 'it was thought quite sufficient.' Others took their duties more seriously yet kept a sense of humour about their task, one, the wit Sydney Smith, claiming his dearest wish was 'to roast a Quaker' just for fun; tongue firmly in cheek, the same parson took up his new parish in Yorkshire in 1809 and reported that, contrary to popular opinion in the south, the people of York wore clothes and were not in fact cannibals.

Bath-night was not a regular occasion in homes as it later came to be – whether this was from laziness or the relatively high price of soap is difficult to tell. Soap is often quoted at ninepence a pound, compared to meat at five- or sixpence; one duchess, on having the dirtiness of her hands pointed out to her, laughed, 'You should see my feet!'. It was John Wesley who revived the old sentiment 'cleanliness is next to godliness', and with good reason – personal hygiene was poor throughout all classes. When wigs were still popular it was considered something of a joke to ruffle one's powdered locks to see how many crawling insects one could precipitate onto a table for amusement, even in mixed company. There is a tale of a wager on a race between two scuttling lice.

Despite the advances made by mechanisation in industry, lighting in the family home did not change much, where the humble candle continued to serve the turn. Some, made of wax, could be expensive but the cheaper varieties of tallow candle, made from rendered animal fat, had a tendency to smell foul as one anonymous writer declared: 'A tallow candle, to be good, must be half Sheep's Tallow and half Cow's; that of hoggs makes 'em gutter, give an ill smell, and a thick black smoak.' Not only was the smoke a problem, but the grease-stains left behind on walls, ceilings, furniture and flooring caused many a servant a hard day's work. In 1783 the Argand lamp (also known as a *colza-oil lamp*, after the thick, greenish-yellow rapeseed oil it burned) was used in some homes, candles not being fully replaced in households until the late 1800s.

Perhaps the poor quality of lighting forced optical science to develop spectacles for the studious – a requisite for reading in the dim of the evening. Reading matter, other than popular novels and the

Playing 'snapdragon': snatching raisins from the snapdragon bowl, 1795. In a darkened room, heated brandy was set alight and the players had to snatch raisins from a bowl and extinguish the fire with their mouths, thereby resembling a dragon.

The cover of *The London Magazine* for August 1779, a 'gentleman's magazine', with news of Parliamentary debate, reviews of the latest books and theatre, and a range of essays.

news-sheets, included the *Gentleman's Magazine*, as well-read as the *London Gazette*, featuring the work of such luminaries as Dr Samuel Johnson, combining political news, satire, town and country affairs, and the latest despatches from officers in the field in time of war. The discovery in 1799 of the Rosetta Stone, key to the translation of the

A Christmas dance in a country home. Such dancing was as common in the nineteenth century as in the eighteenth.

mysterious hieroglyphs of ancient Egypt, was first announced in England in its pages, along with the surrender of French Alexandria to allied British and Ottoman Turkish troops in 1801. It was the eighteenth century's *Punch, Spectator* and *National Geographic* rolled into one, and any gentleman of quality would sit in of an evening to read the latest issue or pore over its tiny print in the annual digest: its pages no larger than those of the present volume, it had two columns of dense type crammed onto each small page.

The greatest family occasion of the year was undoubtedly Christmas, which began on 6 December, St Nicholas' Day, and concluded on Epiphany, on 6 January (Twelfth Night). Middle-class families such as that of Jane Austen set great store by the amounts they gave to charity at this time of year and this was as important as the attendance of distant relations to the household. There was no Christmas tree until the Victorian period, although as a royal tradition the tree was first brought from Germany in 1800 by Queen Charlotte, consort of King George III, and illuminated at Windsor. Turkey, goose, mutton or venison were the common roasts of the day, venison usually taking precedence should such a cut be affordable. Jane Austen wrote to her sister Cassandra in 1807: 'When you receive this our guests will all be gone or going; and I shall be left to the comfortable disposal of my time, to ease of mind from the torments of rice puddings and apple dumplings, and probably to regret that I did not take more pains to please them all.'

Published by William Miller, Albemarle Street, Jan.ʸ 1.ᵗ 1805.

N.º 29.

HOME AND
NEIGHBOURHOOD

L IVING CONDITIONS during these years varied to extremes, but in many ways were still something of an improvement on the desperate state of many agricultural labourers before industrialisation. Life on the land was undoubtedly harsh – the unskilled worker or miner could well have inhabited anything from a leaning shack to a cave, as had been encountered by Daniel Defoe in his *Travels Thro' the Whole Island of Great Britain* earlier in the century. Labourers were paid poor wages, often as low as ten or even eight pence for a twelve-hour day, given ale but no food during their work, and were hired only when needed for specific seasonal tasks, with long periods of unemployment between. However, diarist Gilbert White observed in 1788 that in his Hampshire village of Selborne, where once there had been mud cottages for the poor, they were now housed in homes of brick or stone with 'upstairs bedrooms and glass in the windows'. Pioneering potteries industrialist Josiah Wedgwood recalled similar hardships of those scratching a bare subsistence from the land:

> ... compare this picture, which I know to be a true one, with the present state of the same country; the workers earning nearly double their former wages, their houses mainly new and comfortable, and the lands, roads and every other circumstance bearing evident marks of the most pleasing and rapid improvements.

With the introduction of Watt's steam engine, new factories no longer had to rely upon fast-moving rivers or streams to drive their water-wheels – consequently, where once they had been built in narrow valleys now many were erected in central areas of the towns and cities. The houses that followed these huge buildings, of some 70 or 80 feet in height, were thrown up at so fast a rate that entire streets and new districts were created in a matter of months. Georgian building practices involved the making of bricks on site; however corners were

Opposite:
Two people
changing the
mantle of a gas
lamp, 1808.
The first public
gaslighting was
instituted in
London in 1807,
pioneered by
William Murdoch,
apprentice to
James Watt.

often cut and bricks made from the sweepings of the street, the clay adulterated with mud, earth and horse-dung, and significantly weakened. Walls of many London houses bulged and leaned, floors slewing drunkenly in the years that followed, resulting in dwellings being torn down and rebuilt.

Dr John Aikin described Manchester as it appeared in 1795: 'The new streets built within these few years have nearly doubled the size of the town. Most of them are wide and spacious, with excellent and large houses, principally of brick made on the spot...' But, he complained, many had flights of steps to their front doors which forced pedestrians either to dodge into the as-yet 'unflagged' streets, stumble over them in the dark, or plummet down unseen steps into cellars.

By comparison to later periods Georgian homes were fairly bare, with simple furnishings – though the Prince Regent later started the fashion among the wealthiest for eastern opulence and mimicry of the

A group of people buying and selling 'brown' (unbleached) linen, with a busy market scene. In the background is Banbridge, County Down, Ireland, 1783.

A terrace of farmworkers' cottages in Stamer, near Brighton in East Sussex. The care and attention which has gone into these dwellings is indicative of the importance some landowners placed on their workers' well-being.

Napoleonic 'empire' style. The Manchester homes with the irritating steps mentioned by Dr Aikin would probably have been intended for families that could sustain at least a maid or cook, and might have had loft rooms for servants' beds. However, the house of a doctor could still have been fairly modest: a single staircase with simple handrail and undecorated balusters or plain rods, used by both the family and the servants. In the public rooms there would have been high skirtings, possibly a picture rail above, and shutters at the windows – these had a security function as well as privacy and were held fast by stout catches, their value demonstrated during the food riots of Lancaster and Manchester in the late 1790s.

Though homes were, on the whole, unfussy, the new fad for collecting had begun to clutter up surfaces with ornaments either of antiquarian interest or new items such as Staffordshire pottery figures. This was the age of the gentleman scholar and collector, the amateur scientist and traveller. Collecting had become as widespread among the lower middle classes as among the educated dilettanti of the upper set, and people could demonstrate their fashionable and scholarly pretensions by having local antiquities – or, even better, Greek or Roman relics – displayed in a 'cabinet of curiosities'.

Not all housing was fine. Even before the industrial period Defoe had described Sheffield's streets as 'dark and black' from the smoke, as if forges were always lit, and the French-born American Louis

A general view of the City of London, looking westward and showing old London Bridge, and many ships moored by the Tower, 1794.

Simond, on a tour of factories in 1810–11, compared those of hardware and glassware 'to those of Manchester and Glasgow, which require heat and confined air, and clog the lungs with floating particles of cotton.' The air in northern mill towns was only ever clear on Sundays when the factories were closed. It was Dr Aikin's opinion that the speed with which streets were raised in Manchester was comparable to London. '… So it unfortunately vies with, or exceeds, the metropolis in the closeness with which the poor are crowded in offensive, dark, damp, and incommodious habitations.' He quoted from a committee report on the policing of Manchester: 'In some parts of the town, cellars are so damp as to be unfit for habitations … The poor often suffer from the shattered state of cellar windows. This is a trifling circumstance in appearance, but the consequences to the inhabitants are of the most serious kind.'

It was in this period of early industrialisation that the new slums of northern England were created. Workers' cottages were a very pale imitation of grander homes; their frontages were narrow but having three or possibly four storeys, their rooms stretching deeply to the rear yards and privies. These houses would be let as rooms to families – in the late 1790s a few squalid rooms in London could set a family

The refuse collector, from *Costumes of Great Britain*, 1805.

back 2 shillings and sixpence per week. Many northern mill towns had 'back-to-backs' erected in this period, cramped places which shared a rear yard and party-wall, often with a different family on each floor. The last remaining back-to-backs in Britain are preserved by the National Trust in Birmingham, and were tenanted until 1974.

The sanitary provisions for these areas were grossly inadequate, leading to appalling rates of disease. It was estimated at one point that 250 people were sharing no more than two privies, and the vaults to these were often left open. To empty these vaults and domestic chamber-pots was the unenviable task of the 'night-soilmen' but their work dwindled with the onset of the water-closet. The first practical water-closet was designed by Alexander Cumming in 1775, and this was then improved by Joseph Bramah in 1778; although this model was used for much of the 1800s before the work of Jennings and others, they were largely unsatisfactory and not in widespread use. Dustmen, by contrast to the night-soilmen, emptied ashcans and carted away dustheaps from home fires and braziers; this provided employment for those who were prepared to sift the rubbish, ash and embers for anything of value.

As business in the industrial towns increased, there followed a rise in the number of bankers, lawyers, doctors and other professionals – those who might inhabit the 'handsome' homes described by Aikin in Manchester. The professions have been seen as the bastion of the educated middle classes, but this was a time when people could improve their lot as never before. Many, like William Hutton of Derby,

Willersley Castle, (originally Willersley Hall) in Cromford, Derbyshire, built in the 1780s for famed industrialist Sir Richard Arkwright, the 'father of the factory system'. Arkwright died before its completion, but his son moved into the Hall with his own family in 1796.

began life as apprentices in mills or factories and rose to become wealthy men of status, blurring the lines between the classes. In the mid-eighteenth century, for the cost of several hundred pounds a factory could be built which would later be worth nearly a quarter of a million. The conduct of some of the nouveaux riches was often condemned when they aped their 'betters' by sending their children to expensive boarding schools, or building great country houses for themselves, fitting them out as if for a gentleman. Passable inexpensive imitations of expensive claddings and finishings were conveniently becoming available – yet these were used in wealthy homes too, where economy might oddly pass for fashion: wallpaper could imitate Italian marble while floorboards hidden by a central oriental carpet would remain unvarnished.

In this 'nation of shopkeepers', scant regard was paid at first to the means whereby the shops were stocked. Liverpool was a busy port and the trade centre of northern England, whence bulk orders from the wool or cotton mills departed to continental Europe or India and raw materials arrived from the Orient or the New World. However, not all vessels bore raw materials. In one year alone, 107 slave ships passed through Liverpool's docks, on the 'triangular trade' that took cheap goods to Africa where they were traded for human beings, which were shipped to the Caribbean plantations. Finally the ships returned to Britain, laden with the tobacco or sugar their enforced labour had produced. The stench of these slave ships would waft ashore, the ships rank with the effluent of their wretched cargo who died by the score in the horrifying voyage from Africa or the colonies, the remains of putrefying victims left in shackles beside their terrified brethren. Much of the wealth of Britain in these years was built on this trade, and it was not uncommon to see black faces among the servants of houses, perhaps in livery to please the socially ambitious, and giving a household a touch of the exotic. A few became admired and beloved members of the family – a far cry from their compatriots whose labours kept the nation served with sugar and tobacco, enjoyed by high and low alike, its taint upon virtually every lip across the land.

Opposite: A group of Africans in Surinam are taken to be sold as slaves, 1796. Public awareness of the horrors of slavery was growing as the emancipation campaign gathered pace; it eventually succeeded in 1807.

WORK

E VEN at the height of industrialisation, two-thirds of the population still worked in agriculture – there was no mass exodus from the land into mill towns. It was a gradual process; as land was enclosed and smallholdings sold to squires and land-hungry noblemen, farm labourers were forced to seek work elsewhere – they headed for the industrial centres, established in the mid-1700s. But it was not only the unskilled labourer who suffered.

The gentleman squire was at the top of the local class structure in the countryside, and tenant farmers at the bottom. Just below the squire came the yeoman. The yeomen were pillars of the community, often acting as local overseers, inspectors, occasionally as constables. They had once thrived as owner-occupiers of the farmland – one yeoman commented on a couple that by the end of their days 'they had 400 bullocks', enough money and 'other such stuff' – but in the 1700s the enclosure of their lands drove many into poverty, while the wealth of the landed gentry continued to increase.

Some squires got by on just a few hundred pounds a year to maintain their estate and families, but by the end of the century, land values had doubled and the landed gentry became progressively richer, especially as rising industrial demand for timber and mineral rights brought a windfall to some estates. As the century went on, the more successful country gentlemen might look forward to an annual income of up to £4,000, roughly the equivalent of £380–400,000 today – this when the average labourer's family would exist on barely several shillings per week.

Thanks to industrialisation, there were greater opportunities and a wider variety of work for all members of a family – even children worked for pay from as young as five or six, though in the nineteenth century legislation was brought in banning paid labour younger than nine. Child labour was not a specific evil of the industrial revolution: children had been working on the land and in mines for centuries as

Opposite: Steam engines under construction at the factory of Boulton & Watt at Soho, in Birmingham.

a necessary part of a family's survival. In his memoirs, William Hutton recalled that as a child of seven he was nearly sent to strip tobacco for a grocer, or prepare quills for a weaver, 'but it was at last concluded that I was too young for any employment.' When eventually he was dispatched to work at the silk-mill in his native Derby, he was still considered too young and small to operate the machinery: 'One of the clerks remarked to the person who took me there, that the offer was needless, I was too young. However, the offer was made; and, as hands were wanted, I was accepted ... out of three hundred persons employed in the mill, I was by far the least and the youngest.' He had wooden lifts or pattens tied to each foot to raise him up to the level of the machines; he wore them for an entire year, working from five in the morning until seven at night.

But these children were by no means the hopeless uneducated poor, fit for nothing but drudgery. William's brother, Thomas, by the age of seven knew the 'Jewish history' of the Old Testament and could read Latin, but 'want of bread' sent him to be apprenticed at the mill for eight years, 'Thus a rising genius was cramped, and every prospect of future life clouded.'

Before the tightening of factory law in the 1800s, orphaned children were often provided at a cheap rate by the parish and lodged at factories in crude accommodation, while others were used for much the same reason as by chimney-sweeps, chosen for their size and agility: deadly machinery stood open on the shop floor, exposing workers to untold hazards, and children were often employed specifically because they could fit between equipment either to run messages or for

The picturesque Gibson Mill was tucked in the forested valley of Hardcastle Crags in West Yorkshire, built c. 1800. Originally a cotton mill, it produced fabric until the 1890s and sustained some 21 workers who endured a 72-hour week.

cleaning and maintenance purposes. Small children continued to work in the confined conditions of mines until inspectors and philanthropists raised their voices in protest in the Victorian period.

The lot of women was no better, for they worked alongside men in the factories often for lower pay yet still had to perform domestic tasks at home. This was one of the complaints of factory owners when considering the complications of productivity: 'Many of the Weavers are females, and have cooking, washing, cleaning and various other duties to perform ...' Mining – be it for chalk, lime, iron or lead – threw up its own toxic nightmares, and copper-miners often had green faces from their contact with oxidising copper and succumbed to leakage of poisonous gases within the mine itself. Women, even if not working alongside the men as they certainly did in coal mines, often washed the ore by hand on the surface. They would then carry heavy baskets of ore to be tallied, the baskets often stacked upon their heads. Lead-poisoning was not recognised as a danger to health until the following century (its more noticeable effects, it was believed, were to weaken the wrists and cause a debilitating palsy-like quiver of the knees). Lime is a corrosive agent used at the time for mortar and whitewashing houses but also for sealing bodies in grave-pits; it blisters the skin and causes painful blindness. Cement burns, caused by cement's lime content, were common, as they still are on building-sites today.

Coalbrookdale by night, 1801 by Philip James (Jacques) de Loutherbourg. The glow is of the foundry furnaces, kept burning day and night.

Interior of
a mine in south
Staffordshire. Few
mines were as
spacious as this.

Industrialisation put a great strain on many traditional crafts which had been run from workers' cottages, such as weaving and spinning in particular. When Richard Arkwright produced his first multiple spinning machines such as the 'water-frame' – of comparable efficiency to the famous Spinning Jenny – there was not enough space in the average cottage to house such a thing. Arkwright concentrated his machines in large warehouse-like structures, and these became the 'manufactories'. Many spinners saw the new machines as a threat (not least for taking their industry from their own homes) and James Hargreaves, the lone textile worker who had invented the Spinning Jenny, lost several of his machines in industrial riots: he was forced to flee Blackburn in Lancashire and set up elsewhere. An entire factory was burnt to the ground in Manchester in 1795. Cloth merchants of Leeds, the great wool-producing centre of Britain, had this to say in the public print:

> In the Manufacture of Woollens, the Scribbling Mill, the Spinning Frame, and the Fly Shuttle, have reduced manual Labour nearly One third, and each of them at its first Introduction carried an Alarm to the Work People, yet each has contributed to advance the Wages and to increase the Trade, so that if an Attempt was now made to deprive us of the Use of them, there is no Doubt, but every Person engaged in the Business, would exert himself to defend them.

Weavers had similar arguments against the water-driven power-loom of the 1780s. This was eventually replaced by the steam loom. The argument for the factory-driven steam loom against the output of the home-based hand-loom weaver was incontrovertible, as one inventor recognised:

> A very good Hand Weaver, a man twenty-five or thirty years of age, will weave two pieces of nine-eighths shirting per week, each twenty four yards long ... A Steam Loom Weaver, fifteen years of age, will in the same time weave seven similar pieces. A Steam Loom factory containing two hundred Looms, with the assistance of one hundred persons under twenty years of age, and of twenty-five men will weave seven hundred pieces per week.

In the same report it was calculated that a factory of 200 steam looms could replicate the work of 875 hand looms which would involve roughly 2,000 people. Nevertheless, as the cloth merchants of Leeds pointed out, the new technology expanded the market to the extent that some factories eventually provided employment for some 15,000 people.

Work in a textile factory could begin as early as 5 a.m., and not finish until 9 p.m. Shifts could vary within these times from twelve to sixteen hours: again, not dissimilar to work on a busy farm. Workers were allowed only one hour for lunch, or told to get it while they could, particularly if they were 'thronged' with a big work order. There were no other rest periods, even for stopping to take water. The temperatures in many mills, especially those powered by steam engines, were often greater than 26° C, and exhaustion and heat-stroke were common.

Boys working in a rope-making factory in the 1790s.

Weaving, spinning
and sewing at
home, c. 1770.

The Spinning
Jenny, a multi-
spool spinning
wheel, invented
in 1764 by James
Hargreaves
(1720–78).

Workers had to develop new skills – from Arkwright's weavers and spinners to the potters and porcelain artists in the factories of Josiah Wedgwood, many skilled workers rightly regarded themselves as craftsmen and women and took great pains at their labour. It is impressive that so much quality-based workmanship was carried out at a time of almost continuous change and development, when workers were regularly faced with new and improved machines, bringing with them new methods of operation, new problems and difficulties; between 1780 and 1789 alone, a thousand new patents were registered. Even as late as 1803, after decades of cotton factory production, a new 'dressing frame' was devised which speeded up the weaver's task even more.

One resort for all classes however, was the army. With the French

Revolution in 1789 and subsequent execution of King Louis XVI in 1793, Britain declared war on France in what was later to become the Great French War. It lasted 22 years. The army offered a clean bed, decent regular food and the promise of war-loot, or booty, from the field. Advertising for the Marines offered an immediate payment of 11 guineas for seven years (over £1,200 in today's values) and 16 guineas for 'unlimited service'. One recruitment poster for the Marines called for 'All Dashing and High-Spirited Heroes':

> Good Quarters whilst on Shore; on Board, Plenty of Beef, Pudding and Wine after Dinner. Even these Advantages are trifling when compared to the inestimable one, PRIZE MONEY – Loose [sic] no Time!

With Britain's growing maritime trade fleet which had more than trebled in the eighteenth century from 3,300 ships to nearly 10,000, Britannia ruled the waves – safeguarded by the finest navy in Europe. The Great French War, though a crippling expense, would set Britain on course for unchallenged empire.

Flax heckling, a process that removes impurities from the fibre. This job was previously done by hand with a flat comb.

Next spread: Cotton factories were crowded, noisy and dangerous places with unguarded machinery, beneath which children were expected to clamber to clean. The air was thick with cotton, making it hard to see to the other side of the room.

FOOD AND DRINK

IN A SURVEY OF LONDON it was observed that in working-class districts there was a public house on nearly every street corner, but that these dwindled in number with proximity to areas inhabited by the gentry. The classes were divided on the subject of drink. The factory overseers and owners during the Industrial Revolution were generally of the opinion that there was little point in giving their workers higher wages to keep them motivated in their toil, as this undeserved excess, so it was believed, would only go on drink; according to the medical opinion of George Fordyce in 1793, between bouts of labour the average worker would rest in 'perfect idleness and drunkenness', their women also passing 'very disorderly lives.'

Artist William Hogarth had portrayed the evils of intoxication in his engravings 'Gin Lane' and 'Beer Alley' (both 1750). Beer was favoured over gin, spirits leading to the destruction of society and morals, as Hogarth demonstrated in his art. Beer and ales had for many centuries been popular quenchers, probably safer to drink than water – it would not be for some decades that medicine proved cholera was transmitted through tainted drinking-water. The ale industry was booming and the hops markets of Kent and Sussex were as important as silks and spices from India.

Food became more plentiful with improved crop rotation practices and enclosures offering greater control over arable land. Essays and monographs on food and farming appeared in the learned *Gentleman's Magazine*, such as Sir James Edward Smith's 'Some Observations On the Irritability of Vegetables' of 1788; animal husbandry grew in popularity, enjoying royal patronage from 'Farmer George', the satirical nickname given to King George III. Certain foods made significant contributions to Britain's diet – in particular the potato. A single plant could provide enough food for an entire family; potatoes could be easily stored and would later become a staple diet of the Irish poor. It was, in many ways, a 'potato revolution' which kept industry's

Opposite:
A good meal,
by Thomas
Rowlandson,
with a hefty joint
and plum pudding
washed down
with fortified
wines. No
wonder gout was
such a problem
among the
properous
classes.

A receipt for a three-night stay at the Castle Inn, Preston, in 1808. The stabling cost more than the food bill in the bar.

mills turning. Scottish economist Adam Smith, writing in *The Wealth of Nations* of 1776, observed that an acre could yield '12,000 weight of potatoes' compared to only 2,000 of wheat: '... such an acre of potatoes [even if half were rendered to water] will still produce three times the quantity produced by the acre of wheat,' and 'is cultivated with less expense.'

Smith went on to debate the value of planting wheat, comparing it to oats for making bread, but had misgivings: 'I have been told, that bread of oatmeal is a heartier food for labouring people than wheaten bread, and I have frequently heard the same doctrine held in Scotland. I am, however, somewhat doubtful of the truth of it. The common people in Scotland, who are fed with oatmeal, are in general neither so strong, nor so handsome as the same rank of people in England who are fed with wheaten bread.' David Henry, in *The Complete English Farmer* of 1771, also contrasted potatoes with wheat as a source of flour: 'Certainly, potatoes might be used instead of rye as a substitute for bread, and of this discovery the poor may avail themselves in time of dearth.'

To Adam Smith, potatoes made more commercial sense than wheat. They required more people to cultivate yet the surplus could be fed to the labourers who would then flourish on the diet, increase in population and therefore produce more potatoes – Smith looked upon farm labourers in the same light as factory machines. And potatoes had other benefits: 'The chairmen, porters, and coal-heavers in London, and those unfortunate women who live by prostitution, the strongest men and the most beautiful women perhaps in the British dominions, are said to be the greater part of them from the lowest rank of people in Ireland, who are generally fed with this root.'

Local markets were the source of all supplies, and few towns in Britain were without some form of district or central marketplace, such as the covered market still in existence in Oxford today. Butcher, baker and, at times doubtless candlestick-maker too, could be found under one roof. The householder could also obtain supplies from the hawkers and pedlars who went from door to door in the densely populated towns, where they found plenty of custom.

The cost of food varied as commodities dictated by the fluctuations at the local corn exchange, and from region to region or even parish to parish. However, in the period 1780–1835 the following prices were roughly the average:

bread	1d–4d per lb
butter	9d–1s per lb
sugar	6d per lb
meat	5d–8d per lb
beer	1d per pint
tea	10s–20s per lb
oatmeal	2d per lb
potatoes	½ d per lb
soap	6d per lb

As William Hutton recalled of hunger on his travels, 'If a man has any money, he will see stalls enough in London which will supply him with something to eat; and it rests with him to lay out his money to the best advantage … The next morning I breakfasted in Smithfield, upon furmity, [a dish of wheatmeal with nuts and fruit, similar to

Boy and fruit-woman. Itinerant fruit sellers were a regular feature of the urban scene.

The Wheatshief (sic) Eating House, Salisbury Court, Fleet Street, by Thomas Rowlandson.

A kitchen scene, painted by John Atkinson, 1771.

muesli or porridge] at a wheelbarrow. Sometimes I had a halfpenny-worth of soup, and another of bread. At other times bread and cheese.'

Some dwellings had less than adequate cooking facilities – for them the solution was the cookshop or tavern. The cookshops had declined in appeal to the more discerning client by the 1770s, sited as they were in poorer quarters of town and catering as they did for people with only a few pence to spare. Taverns provided more expensive fare; some would cook cuts of meat for customers, much as Samuel Johnson once enjoyed his 'meat pye' in such a hostelry as 'one could attend it' personally. The last resort was to pick up a snack from the street-traders with mobile food stalls offering titbits from meats to roast chestnuts.

The eating regimes of the upper and middle classes were appalling by modern health standards. Characters in Jane Austen novels often take long morning walks of several miles before having a light breakfast at 10 a.m. This often consisted of bread and butter, possibly cheese or the wonder of the Europeans, English toast: 'There is a way of roasting slices of buttered bread before the fire which is incomparable,' wrote Karl Philipp Moritz in his travels through Britain in the 1780s. The typical gentleman's residence would then provide a dinner heavily favouring meats, including pies, fowl, loin and fillet of veal, legs of lamb and roast pork, boiled beef and plum puddings; in the early 1700s this meal was eaten as early as 2 p.m., but in the 1780s and 1790s this moved to 5 p.m. and later 7 p.m. The exertions of business pushed professionals, factory owners and overseers to eat according to business hours – from this, luncheon gradually developed, a meal taken somewhere in the middle of the day. Dinner would be followed by a supper which could often be taken anywhere from 9 p.m. to 2 a.m. depending on a gentleman's habits. These habits included long drinking sessions after a meal, when the ladies excused themselves to the drawing-room, and the men carried on, breaking the rhythm of their drinking perhaps to relieve themselves in chamber-pots kept in the sideboard.

Game might have been marginally more plentiful in the countryside than in the towns, but with the enclosure of lands in many regions, access to game was restricted – old hunting-grounds now became the haunt of poachers, driven to crime by necessity; it soon became a criminal offence to own a hunting firearm, even if for protection. Hunting occupied many young gentlemen almost every day. Whether on horse or on foot, armed with the finest flintlock rifle-musket by such famed gunmakers as Joseph Manton, their need for game descended almost to the level of a hobby – though many large estates managed their game stocks so well that hunting became a source of employment for estate workers.

There was an abundance of food, and the nature of farming became a science, with livestock bulging into prize-winning proportions. Through international trade and the Caribbean plantations there were new foods in increased supply at lower prices, helping the lowest on the social scale to survive. Gluttony became a sport for some, the Prince Regent himself becoming famously fat to the amusement of his often disgusted courtiers. Yet, even with the growth of the national stewpot, and 'John Bull's Beef', the poor could still starve in the streets, as the wealthy 'people of quality' continued to dine.

A hawker holds up rabbits to be inspected by the lady of the house. This engraving dates from 1792 (before the abolition of slavery). Although the hawker is well dressed it is not clear if he is a free man, an employee, or the property of an overseer.

S. B. Litchfield, Fruiterer & Confectioner – a business card for a purveyor not only of fresh fruit, but of ices, jellies and soups.

Shopping and Style

NAPOLEON was right in many ways when he referred to Britain as a 'nation of shopkeepers', for few countries in Europe at the time could compete with the entrepreneurial merchants of the British Isles. The average small town boasted a host of services – a population of 1,500 would support half a dozen blacksmiths, carters, possibly a cooper, several drapers, haberdashers, tailors, milliners, bakers, butchers, grocers and chemists. Some of these would sell other goods as well as their mainstay, such as the draper selling groceries – one village shop in Sussex, Turner's, was a combined draper's, grocer's, hatter's, ironmonger's and stationer's. Many small towns also had chandlers, coal and timber merchants, not to mention the normal number of hawkers and pedlars who would call at the back door of every household. If there were no butcher, fishmonger or grocer, it would only be because such perishables were provided by regular street-markets, a vital lifeline of supplies.

Specialist shops providing linens, haberdashery or furnishings survived for decades owing to a relatively unchanging demand for certain fashion items, though innovations created markets for new goods – women's underwear, for example was introduced on a wide scale to Britain after the 1780s owing only to a fashionable adjustment of dress style. Women's fashions in the Industrial Revolution became simpler and straighter until, in what became known as the neoclassical French 'Empire' style in the early nineteenth century, the waistline rose to fit under the bust. This made the 'shift' or 'smock', which had been the chief undergarment of the earlier age, too bulky to wear, and called for new Continental underwear. These long-legged French 'drawers' or 'knickers' were later replaced again by pantaloons and pantalettes, which had drawstrings at the knee.

These developments were supported by the textile factories which produced soft cottons and muslins, fabrics much favoured by English dressmakers. Although weaving and spinning had once been the

Opposite:
'Be not amaz'd dear Mother,
It is indeed your daughter Anne': a cartoon mocking the fashion for big wigs, 1774.

Young woman in a flowing shift with tie-belt, 1802.

cottage industries of the working class, many women of the educated middle classes often took up needle and thread themselves, making their own clothes from the ready supply of fabrics obtained from the local haberdasher. Any saving for the family of an unmarried woman was no bad thing. As the novels of Jane Austen indicate (she herself being no stranger to needlework), sewing was not considered too lowly a task for ladies of genteel birth – though having sufficient funds to pay for the services of a professional couturier with access to the latest fashions was of course preferable.

Men's fashions too became simpler and more clean-lined, though a frill at the shirt-front and cravat was always desirable, the exposed throat covered by the standing collar and long wraparound 'stock' either in black or white. This was the day of the 'dandy' Beau Brummel, who is later credited with designing the gentleman's suit and tie, with revolutionary long trousers instead of

'Two ladies in the most fashionable dejeuner dresses of the year 1784'.

the traditional knee-breeches and stockings. The tall sixteenth- and seventeenth-century over-the-knee boot, often turned down into broad flaps, became simplified into the turned-down huntsman's boot, showing a tan lining at the top of a black leather outer, a vestige of its former swagger. The bouffon powdered wig of the white-faced aristocrat, so often portrayed in images of the French Revolution and the satirical cartoons of Thomas Rowlandson, became less popular with the active gentlemen of the 1790s, who liked to spend their time out exploring, touring or hunting. It lost its popularity not just for fashion reasons (or indeed for health reasons), but largely because in 1795 Prime Minister William Pitt, in a desperate attempt to finance the war against France, taxed the fine white powder used to whiten men's wigs.

Many shopkeepers lived above or inside their shops, some sleeping on cots beside their wares or by their looms, cutting-benches and counters. Nevertheless, as commercial awareness grew, many shopowners tried to make their displays more appealing, gilding their shopfronts, shaping eye-catching displays, be it of lamps, pottery or 'pyramids of pineapples, figs, grapes, oranges and all manner of fruits'. Wedgwood's emporium in the West End of London was a symphony of

Inside view of the drapers Messrs. Harding, Howell, and Co. 89, Pall Mall, 1809.

Fashion before ease, or a good constitution sacrificed for a fantastic form. This cartoon by Hannah Humphrey, 1793, is a political comment on the Jacobin threat, but it also demonstrates the use of corsets in the 1790s before the move to the looser French 'Empire' dress styles.

Opposite top: A Stamp Office certificate for annual duty for hair powder, 1799.

polished wood floors, pillared and plastered ceilings in the new neoclassical style, with vases and bowls displayed enticingly on shelves, the displays rearranged each day to please the eye. It was his mission to 'amuse and divert, please, astonish, nay, even to ravish the Ladies'.

Wedgwood won a high place in London Society, becoming a Fellow of both the Royal Society and the Society of Antiquaries in the 1780s. At the other end of the social spectrum was the unskilled labourer on paltry wages; such a man would do little shopping on Wedgwood's lavish premises. The wage of such a figure, living on what was regarded as the subsistence level, tended to be between a mere penny and twopence an hour, according to region and often according to parish. Even this was considerably higher than that received by workers doing similar jobs in Ireland. A weekly wage of 7 shillings and sixpence to 10 shillings was common; 15 shillings was good. By contrast a busy weaver could hope for a grand 25 shillings per week (£1 5s). It was for these reasons that an entire family would work, children included. Bearing in mind the cost of food, there would have been little left over for such families to spend at the haberdasher's or shoemaker's.

This was not the only problem faced at the lower levels of commerce. Counterfeit currency was everywhere, with many silver coins thin, worn and clipped by 'coin-clippers' — who would melt down the clippings for solid sterling — but an endemic shortage of copper coinage became a problem for people living on pennies at the lower end of the economy. King George III had declined to have his image struck upon copper coins by the Royal Mint as it was a base metal, and undeserving of such lofty patronage. Consequently,

Below: The local squire gives out charity to those at his gate, late eighteenth century.

Women and
children in an
English dressing
room, 1789.

supplies of copper coins were only irregularly renewed. To counteract this, unofficial copper coins abounded in provincial regions which instituted a system of tokens. These copper tokens often depicted such stirring images as a galloping trooper of the local yeomanry cavalry militia, and looked just as fine as any other of the realm. They might be accepted as currency in a particular locality, or might be issued by a factory owner for use in his tied shop.

Taxes also whittled away at the working man's coin. A hawker, who earned his trade by going from door to door selling clothing, textiles and all sorts of other goods, had to obtain a licence; this cost him the gargantuan sum of £4 – if he had a horse, this was doubled to £8, equivalent to a month's wages for an unskilled labourer. Even these rates were raised temporarily in the late 1780s, when shopkeepers waged a campaign to remove the threat that these peripatetic traders posed to their own businesses. Shopkeepers were themselves assessed in ingenious ways: tax on a shopkeeper in premises with seven windows and an annual rent of £6 in 1797 was 18 shillings and twopence. Worse was suffered by a shopkeeper in premises of 23 windows with an annual rent of £50, especially if he kept a servant and, oddly, a dog: his tax bill came to £12 14s. The gentry were similarly penalised: in 1777 they had to pay a tax of one guinea for each male servant in their household, and 10 shillings on each gold watch (excluding the first).

What cash a Briton had in his pocket seemed to be spent readily in the shops of the nation; the cost of living rose to keep pace: from 1785 to 1797 a pound of wheat flour nearly quadrupled from 1¾ pence to 4½ pence. The average working Englishman's tax bill in 1776 was £1 5s, but by 1797 a York shopkeeper was paying as much as £4. Business was booming, the fortunes of men rising, industry flourishing and everywhere the increase of merchandise, money and spending. Small wonder that Britain developed a taste for the luxuries of tea and porcelain from China and the riches of the Honourable East India Company, sent back to Liverpool and Bristol in the groaning holds of armed East Indiamen merchant ships. After 1795, two years into the war with revolutionary France, British troops seized the Cape of Good Hope on the southern tip of Africa, guaranteeing a safe passage to India and barring the way to the French. The result was a steady flow of silks, gold, gemstones and raw spices in the midst of war. The values are difficult to comprehend at a time of manifest poverty, but the jewelled spoils taken from the palace of the defeated Tipu Sahib at Seringapatam in 1799 amounted to nearly £2 million when they were auctioned off – the equivalent of over £20 million today.

TRANSPORT

BRITAIN'S ROAD NETWORK at the beginning of the 1700s was second to none, but the state of these roads was abysmal. Travellers high and low complained of ruts so deep they would regularly overturn coaches, and forming what would be in summer a staggering series of jolting hillocks but in winter a quagmire of 'spue and mud', sinking a carriage up to its axles. Economics changed this in the Industrial Revolution, when the poor state of the roads became a hurdle to the steady flow of commerce, not least to stagecoaches, whose routes criss-crossed the country with a regularity that might put some services to shame today.

There was no national authority to oversee these changes; instead they were enacted by Turnpike Trusts. Major highways were maintained by toll-keepers who charged travellers for the use of their stretch of road. They lived an often isolated existence in a toll-house, positioned on a bridge or gateway at the city limits, sometimes armed with a barrier, its authority perhaps reinforced by the blast of a musket. Even Prime Minister William Pitt and the Lord Chancellor were once on the receiving end of a salvo, having passed through a toll-gate without paying: thinking Pitt and his fellows a gang of highwaymen, the outraged toll-keeper let rip with a bell-muzzled blunderbuss, but luckily caused no damage.

By the 1780s there were 15,000 miles of taxed turnpike roads, each one earning its keep according to its traffic – though there were so many exemptions for these tolls the onus fell most heavily upon the already overburdened labourer, merchant and farmer. The tolls were so unpopular and so unjust that toll-keepers were often attacked, their barriers destroyed and their cashboxes looted: there is a tale of a

Opposite and below: Pontcysyllte aqueduct in north Wales, the longest and highest in Britain, and raising the Llangollen Canal over the Dee Valley, was completed in 1805.

Right: London and Exeter post-coach, details of carriage, times and costs; the journey took a day and a half, and luggage followed in a separate carriage which took a few hours longer. The first mail coaches ran on this route ran in 1784.

LONDON and **EXETER** **POST-COACH,**
At **TWO POUNDS** each.
Short Paſſengers at **THREE-PENCE HALFPENNY** per Mile.

THE Proprietors beg Leave to return their Thanks to the Nobility and Gentry for the kind Indulgence ſhewn them in preferring their Coach to any other; and in order to accommodate thoſe who wiſh to travel ſtill more expeditious,

A STAGE-CHAISE

Sets out from the Saracen's Head, in Friday-Street, LONDON; and from the London Inn, in EXETER, every Morning at Six o'Clock, and arrives at each of the above Places the next Day at Noon. It carries THREE PASSENGERS, at 2l. 4s. each. The Turnpikes and Boys paid by the Proprietors. Each Perſon allowed 14l. Luggage, and no more; all above may be ſent by the Poſt Coach, which arrives the ſame Evening.

A GENTEEL CHAISE

Is likewiſe provided on the ſame Terms to go from EXETER to PLYMOUTH, and back again, every Day;—ſets out at Six o'Clock every Morning from Exeter and Plymouth.

Proprietors, { J. LAND, London Inn, EXETER.
{ J. HAYES, King's Arms, CHUDLEIGH.
{ J. BICKNELL, Prince George, PLYMOUTH.

COLLINS & JOHNSON,   PRINTERS, SALISBURY.

Below: The morning after the masquerade; a lady is carried homeward in a sedan chair, eighteenth century.

400-strong mob in Somerset descending on a single toll-house, dispersed only by the dragoon cavalry.

Despite abuses of the system, such as when the toll-keeper pocketed extra cash by falsifying the number of passages under his barrier, the state of the roads improved to such an extent that travelling times fell dramatically. Where it had taken 50 hours of bone-jolting coach travel from Norwich to London at the beginning of the eighteenth century, by 1800 it took only 19; similarly the agonising 90 hours faced by textile tycoons in Manchester on a journey to London was reduced to just over 30. These improvements were achieved through a combination of improved roads and technology. Whereas carriages had been slung from thick leather straps between axles – the consequent nauseating sway can only be imagined – these were replaced by new industrial metal springs, the original of the system still in use today. However, turnpikes made travel expensive: in 1774 it cost £4 8s to go from Oxford to London (over £40 today). In 1769 a coach fare from Scotland to London cost £7, and in 1800 the same journey was double. This is

A groom holding
a carriage team,
painted by Clifton
Tomson (1775–
1828).

considerably higher than the standard stage-coach rate of 2d a mile in
winter and 3 ½d a mile in summer.

Despite the improvements, riding on a stagecoach was still far
from pleasant. Seats were not always available – it was common
practice to climb onto the roof and cling to a small hand-grip. This
exposed the traveller to all weathers, and the likelihood of a long fall
should the coach lurch and overturn in a rut, or with the loss of a
wheel the luggage, held in a basket beside him, tumbling out and
crashing against him. Long journeys inevitably involved an overnight
stay at a roadside inn; German novelist Karl Philipp Moritz

*The Waggoner's
Rest*, a roadside
inn, by Thomas
Rowlandson,
c. 1800–05.

complained bitterly about his stay at one where he was obliged by a snide chambermaid to share a bedroom with a stranger – it was located right above the main saloon. 'The floor shook. There were drinking-songs' and when eventually he managed to get to sleep his roommate stumbled in, blundering his way to his bed where he collapsed, boots and all, into a snoring chorus. The staff were rude, one waiter regarding his tip with a 'God damn you sir!' and his little chambermaid had the effrontery to ask for a tip herself, 'Pray remember the chambermaid!' whereupon Moritz doubtless took some pleasure in replying: '"Yes, yes," said I, "I shall long remember your most ill-mannered behaviour and shameful incivility," and gave her nothing.

On top of all this, for a hundred years or more the traveller had to contend with the scourge of the roads: the highwayman. The Industrial Revolution period saw little change in the activities of highwaymen, though there was perhaps a slight drop in their numbers owing to increased business opportunities in other fields. Many of them claimed to be 'gentlemen in distress' forced into their dark deeds by economic necessity. The highwayman was often romanticised as the noble but unfortunate masked gentleman-thief politely relieving enthralled ladies of their purses. It was said that some gallantly escorted their victims along dangerous stretches of road to see they were not robbed again, and then ensured they had sufficient funds to continue their journey – perhaps in exchange for not appearing as witnesses against the marauder 'should he come to it'. Many were not so chivalrous, ready to murder on the slightest provocation, and some had the gall to distribute a general warning around wealthy districts of London not to pass through certain areas of the countryside without at least 10 guineas and a gold watch ready to hand over – 'on pain of death'.

The chief development of the period with regard to the highwayman was technological,

These stagecoach passengers have disembarked to wade through the quicksands near Woburn. The coach guard's blunderbuss is clearly depicted. 1796 cartoon by Cruikshank.

seen in the weaponry used by both bandits and coachmen. Gunplay was not uncommon, highwaymen being compelled to shoot at a driver to stop him making an escape. When the coachman returned fire, travellers and escorts could easily lose their lives. Flintlock pistols were just as deadly as their modern counterparts, some with calibres of nearly half an inch, larger than most military firearms of today. For the coachman, the blunderbuss was ideal. Its wide-mouthed muzzle was not designed to scatter shot, as many suppose, but to make it more threatening and easy to load – firearms of the day were all muzzle-loaders, requiring powder, ball and wadding to be rammed down the barrel. The yawning mouth of the blunderbuss (from the Dutch *donderbus*: 'thunder-box') could be loaded even while a coach was juddering across a rutted road. Its consequent blast was often so powerful it is credited with taking half a man's midsection away on impact. Other developments included the gentleman's pocket-pistol, specially designed for self-defence in coach travel; the other technological marvel was the 'pepperbox' pistol, with multiple hand-rotated barrels, some eventually capable of sixteen shots. With such a pistol, a gentleman could bring down one man after another without reloading or having to draw another pistol. These handguns were soon mass-produced after their inception in the 1790s, and later became the revolvers of today.

The economy of the nation was dependent, however, more on the canal system than the road network. The industrialisation of Manchester, it was observed, was due almost entirely to the canal which supplied it with coal. The architect of this link was John Brindley; his Bridgewater Canal is viewed as the first truly artificial waterway in Britain. Commissioned in 1759, it was opened in 1761 and shipped coal from the mines of the Duke of Bridgewater at Worsley to Manchester; it needed no locks but included an aqueduct to cross the River Irwell. With the introduction of steam power in the city, the canal became vital, supplying the factory furnaces with fuel. Previously, like the road network, waterways had been inefficient

This Dublin-marked British musketoon is an example of the blunderbuss-style gun, the most popular weapon of the English coachman in the late eighteenth century. Like all other weapons of the day, these were loaded from the muzzle with powder, ball and wadding, then rammed and packed tightly in the barrel ready for firing.

Next spread: The canals required heavy investment to build but made it possible to transport heavy goods cheaply and quickly. By the 1830s, almost 4,000 miles of waterways had been built. Barges were pulled by horses from the towpath, and a community of canal dwellers soon emerged.

The title-page picture of a pamphlet on two recent disasters at sea, 1780s.

means of transport, often needing to be widened and deepened to allow larger craft to negotiate their narrow banks. Brindley went on to devise the Grand Trunk Canal which connected all of the major river routes of central England.

Canals permitted the reliable transport of heavy goods and raw materials, and the demand for these new waterways is evident: from 1761 to 1790 roughly £60,000 was spent on canal digging, but in the next decade expenditure on canal construction rose to over £750,000 each year. For most of the second half of the eighteenth century Parliamentary approval had been granted for one or two canals to be built annually, but in 1793–94 alone, 30 canal projects were launched. Canals were part of the first industrial transport revolution, but were soon to be overtaken by another, propelled by Watt's steam engine.

Railways had their origins in mining, the wagonways of coal mines using wooden rails to support four-wheeled trucks to cart ore out of the pit and return empty, eventually without the use of horsepower to draw them out. These wooden rails wore out after prolonged use and were often topped by a protective metal strip – it was not long before industry saw the value of fashioning these out of solid iron: the first all cast-iron rails were constructed at Coalbrookdale in1767 and wrought-iron rails followed in 1808. Although many of these systems existed in northern mining areas, the south too had its 'wagonways', the first all-metal railway was built in Surrey, from Wandsworth to Croydon, in 1801.

Rolling Carts and Waggons.

TO afcertain the Advantages of thefe Waggons, a few Journies have been made into *Warwickfhire* and *Staffordfhire*; about thirty Journies to *Bedford*; and, on the 3d of November laft, they began going from *Whittlebury Foreft* to *Northampton*, about fourteen Miles, and continued without Intermiffion every Day, till the latter end of *March* following, with fuch heavy Loads of Timber, that fome People fuppofed the Road would have been deftroyed by fuch conftant Carriage in wet Weather (it not being ufual in this Country to carry Timber in Winter Months) but the contrary Effect was remarkaby proved by the Ufe of Rolling Waggons, and the Road, fo far from being injured, was a very extraordinary Sight, the Quarters formed by the Rollers, both in the private Roads and Turnpikes, were fo even and flat as to make an excellent Paffage for Horfes abreaft, or any Kind of quartering Carriages, and fo fmooth and clean, 'that even foot Paffengers preferred them to walking in the Fields, and the Road being thus rolled, enabled the Cattle to draw much heavier Loads than are ufually carried in fo deep a Country.

The good Effects of Rollers were fo apparent during the Winter, that Advertifements were frequently inferted in all the *London* News-papers; that the Public might view the Carriages and their Effects, while they were at Work in the Neighbourhood of *Northampton* and *Stony Stratford*.

Mr. William James and Son, Proprietors of the *Bath* and *Briftol* Waggons, had their firft Rolling Waggon in the beginning of *Auguft* laft, which fet out for *Briftol* with a larger Load than is ufually carried upon that Road; and it was found to anfwer fo well, upon its firft Journey, that more Rolling Waggons are now building for Mr. James, and there is no Doubt but he will foon find them profitable to himfelf, as well as ferviceable to the Public.

The following Encouragement is allowed by the two late Acts of Parliament to Carriages upon this Conftruction.

BY an Act for the Amendment and Prefervation of the public Highways,' all Carriages, moving upon Rollers of the Breadth of fixteen Inches, are allowed to be drawn with any Number of Horfes, or other Cattle. And,

By an Act for regulating the Turnpike Roads,' fuch Waggons are allowed to carry eight Tons in Summer, and feven Tons in Winter, and may be drawn with any Number of Horfes or other Cattle.

They are alfo permitted to pafs upon any Turnpike Road, TOLL-FREE, for the Term of one Year, to be computed from *Michaelmas*, 1773; and, after the Expiration of the faid Term, fhall pafs upon any Turnpike Road, through any Toll-Gate or Bar, for Half Toll.

This Encouragement to Rollers, together with the feveral Reftraints laid upon Nine Inch as well as Narrow Wheels, by thefe Acts, make it the Intereft of all People to put their heavy Carriages upon Rollers, which cannot fail of making every Road in the Kingdom perfectly fmooth. It will then be found that every Horfe will draw much more than he now does; for it is well known that upon rail'd Roads that are level (where Waggons move upon a frame of Wood) almoft any Horfe is able alone to draw four Tons, merely becaufe the Road is made a Part of the Mechanifm, which every Road ought to be; and which defirable Effect nothing but Rollers can produce.

Upon the Whole, both Carts and Waggons, upon this Conftruction, are found by Experience to anfwer every Purpofe that can be defired, even in the very worft of Roads: They are both cheaper and much lighter than common Nine-inch Broad Wheels; they are more durable, and are fure to produce a fmooth Road.

Great Variety of Rolling Carriages, and alfo Garden and Land Rollers of a new Conftruction, are ready for Infpection.

N. B. Rolling Carts and Waggons of all Kinds, according to Act of Parliament, are built by JAMES SHARP, of *Leadenhall-Street, London.*

The application of the Boulton & Watt steam engine to these new 'rail ways' was attempted in 1794 when William Murdoch, Watt's assistant, devised a successful steam engine which could propel itself, a 'locomotive' – but this, for unknown reasons, was not supported by the company and shelved. Instead, the first steam railway in Britain was constructed in Wales, at Merthyr Tydfil, by Richard Trevithick, in 1804. It was not successful, but it set the scene for passenger travel: in 1806 a horse-drawn railway began operating from Swansea to The Mumbles – however, the steam engine did not graduate successfully to rail travel for another ten years, a task masterminded by the 'Father of the Railway', George Stephenson.

Rolling carts and wagons, with wheels up to 16 inches wide, were encouraged in the 1770s as providing a more effective way of hauling heavy loads, with less damage to the road surface, and with less strain on the horses. To encourage their use, they were exempted from tolls for a year.

ENTERTAINMENT

O F ALL THE PASTIMES most associated with Georgian Britain, gambling seems the most predominant. It touched on all classes, from the farmhands gathering to watch ratting in the barn to the gentry at the racetrack or gaming table. With the economic boom, the moneyed classes seemed to be more willing than ever to part with their cash. 'Fashion was less concerned with culture than with cockfights, the prize ring and the set of a coat.' Gambling became more than a harmless vice, and it was not unknown for entire estates to change hands at the cut of a deck of cards; it affected both sexes equally, with one noble chatelaine falling into a debt of over £30,000. Men had to be banned from wearing swords in the fashionable 'Pantiles' area of Tunbridge Wells, owing to the escalating number of duels and hot-blooded murders between angry card-players.

Reading was more popular than many now suppose. With the widespread use of printing, more and more books were published than ever before; novels in multiple volumes were eagerly snatched off the shelves, some being read in the streets before they were displayed in shops. Popular non-fiction included learned tomes, travellers' diaries and sporting books, chief among the latter's subjects being hunting and racing.

Fox-hunting now became a national obsession; clergymen might deliver their sermons while wearing hunting-boots under their cassocks – some had been known to hurry to their mounts, abandoning their congregations, as soon as sight of a fox had been made. The years 1780–1800 are regarded as the heyday of the fox-hunt, King George III having been a very keen huntsman. There were hunts around London, such as the annual meeting in Epping Forest and others at Muswell Hill and Enfield Chase to the north of the city. Hare-coursing or greyhound-coursing was another popular sport in the countryside, led by the exclusivity of Lord Orford's coursing club in 1776: in an aristocratic affectation typical of this age, membership was limited to the number of letters in the alphabet, each hound being

Opposite:
To the Society of Goffers [golfers] *At Blackheath.* Mr William Innes, merchant, plays golf on the heath, 1790.

Breakfast before the hunt; fox- hunters carousing, by Thomas Rowlandson, c. 1785–90.

named after his appropriate letter – when a member died or retired, his place was filled by ballot.

With the rise of the wealthy industrialist, though, hunting was no longer the exclusive preserve of the upper classes and became associated with 'rough manners'; it was often frowned upon by the more studious gentleman who would take more to angling, or wildfowling with flintlock musket or, later, rifle. Duck-hawking, a medieval country sport, carried on at the end of the century. Even so, well-bred society looked down their noses at such pursuits, as Lord Chesterfield wrote to his godson:

> Eat as much game as you please, but I hope you will never kill any yourself; and indeed, I think you are above any of these rustick, illiberal sports of guns, dogs and horses, which characterise our English Bumpkin Country Gentleman.

There was always fencing, or dancing for the polite gentleman, dancing being regarded as something of an exercise as well as a mating ritual, displaying the attributes of a young man to a host of ladies while testing the stamina as well; the famous 'Hornpipe' dance of the Royal Navy was a method of keeping crews fit at sea and occasionally served as a mass punishment aboard ship. Quieter outdoor games such as bowls and quoits were very popular for the genteel, each providing ample opportunity for betting. Archery had all but vanished except as a pastime for ladies, and rose in prominence as such in the 1800s. Women took part in sports towards the end of the eighteenth century; the satirical caricatures of 'Miss Trigger' and 'Miss Wicket' were well known from 'The Sporting Lady' of 1776:

> Miss Trigger you see, is an excellent shot
> And forty-five notches Miss Wicket has got!

Women were depicted playing cricket [hence 'Miss Wicket'], and the lower elements engaged in bare-knuckle boxing or simple all-out brawls in darkened corners of Clerkenwell, where butchers and porters would thrash out their differences as well. Boxing became a very popular sport among young gentlemen, and seemed the second-most popular pastime after hunting. For a quieter time, billiards was another excellent sport, and often another means of gambling.

Boxing, Mendoza v. Humphry, 1796; gloves or 'mufflers' were not introduced until the nineteenth century.

Cricket being played at The Royal Academy Club in Marylebone Fields, eighteenth century.

Traditional sports of the working man were still common, such as football, wrestling and 'cudgel-playing'. The cockpit still lured gamblers to place their bets on the fierce gamecocks, their armament augmented by steel barbs, though this particular blood sport was banned in the nineteenth century.

Village fairs with their regular attractions of wrestling matches and games were the traditional method of keeping country folk in contact, just as church fairs and annual get-togethers or dances at the local Assizes did, and these suffered little change as the century neared its close. For most however, horse-racing held the greatest appeal. Defoe had complained of the loose morals at work in Newmarket; pickpocketing, drinking, rowdy behaviour and gambling whereby a man might lose a thousand guineas one day and win two thousand the next. Newmarket, Ascot, Doncaster and Epsom were all favoured courses, popular with all levels of society (the Epsom Derby was first run in 1779 as a race to find the best three-year-old in the land). Book-making was common in gentlemen's clubs, one such dating back to 1775, but it was legitimised as a profession when a certain William Ogden made it into a business in 1793.

Evening relaxation among the gentry and the new would-be gentry involved the after-dinner pleasures of music, conversation and, for the unattached chaperones, cards. Every well-educated lady would have some schooling on the harpsichord or, later, the piano; many of Jane Austen's novels include scenes of whispered gossip in the drawing-room where the hopeful suitor would contrive to be the page-turner of the sheet music for his paramour at the piano. Either that or the couple could 'take exercise', which usually meant several turns around the room at a strolling pace, to keep conversation from other small groups scattered about on sofas and settles. If this were not sufficient the gentry had the two great outdoor venues of the London 'season' at Vauxhall and Ranelagh Gardens, to attend for dancing, dining and an evening of theatre. Such events often featured fireworks and had the air of a grand fair. The greatest single public event of the day was perhaps the balloon ascent of Vincenzo Lunardi in September 1784; not only did he take flight but he was equipped with one of the first known parachutes. Lunardi's balloon trip, from City Road in London, is believed to be the period's largest gathering of people at any single event, the crowd estimated to have numbered some two hundred thousand. He rose to a great height, and came safely to earth again some distance to the north, at Ware in Hertfordshire.

Of all the recreations, the theatre gained most prominence as the towns grew. No longer were theatre troupes forced to travel from village to village, performing on feast days or at fairs, though many still did; instead provincial theatres began to cater for steadily increasing audience numbers; from 1769–77, royal theatres were built in Bath, Norwich, York, Hull, Liverpool and Chester, and sixpence could buy a seat in the gallery. The great theatres of London such as the Haymarket and Theatre Royal were well established, David Garrick's performances among the most popular. Vast numbers attended, Drury Lane seating over 3,500 after its renovation in 1794 and Covent Garden taking 3,000. In the middle

Engraving of David Garrick as the title character in Shakespeare's *Macbeth*. By Charles White, 1775.

A fairground merry-go-round, with children playing with wooden toys as they wait for their turn.

An orchestra plays from an illuminated bandstand at Vauxhall Gardens, playground of the well-to-do.

of the century it was estimated over 12,000 attended the theatre each week. A play could form only part of an evening's programme, much more like a night of variety than today's one-performance theatre; a playbill 'The Polish Tyrant' followed by displays of 'Skill on the Slack-Rope' and yet another play 'The Genius of the Wood'.

Other than comedies of manners, revived tragedies and histories, one of the most popular forms of theatre was the pantomime, a peculiar combination of silent mime, opera and dramatic sets providing 'dark rocky caverns by the side of a Wood, illumin'd by the Moon' and 'flashes of lightning' – the favourite hero was Harlequin from the Italian *Commedia dell'Arte*. In the 1770s spoken dialogue was introduced to these shows but audiences demanded the former magic of silence, and in 1786 the dumb-show returned. The audience was not to be denied: they were inevitably rowdy, drunken and dangerous, gentlemen duelling in the aisles, fist-fights breaking out in the stalls or the pit, while prostitutes patrolled the boxes, servicing the lords while they huzzahed the hero or booed the villain, the whole scene occasionally descending into riot, tearing the theatre to pieces. Spectators in the gallery often flung rubbish, food or glasses of drink over the audience in the stalls below, the safest tactic being to wear one's hat; 'such outrages are committed in the name of freedom' said one foreign visitor in his disgust.

As the century drew to a close, audiences became better behaved – some refraining altogether from applause until the curtain-call – and theatre grew from the public bear-pit which it had been to an evening of refined appreciation of acting skill. Possibly it lost something of its appeal to the ordinary working man or woman, though there were always venues to provide a welcome respite from a harsh reality for all.

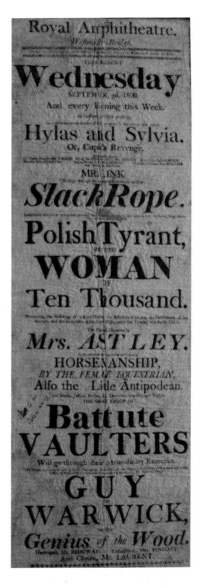

A single night's entertainment at the Royal Amphitheatre, 1806, combining plays, acrobatics and song.

EDUCATION AND SOCIAL SERVICE

THE CONCEPT OF EDUCATING the working population was by no means universally accepted. 'It is safest for both the government and religion of the country to let the lower classes remain in that state of ignorance, in which nature has originally placed them,' said the Lord Bishop of London in 1803. Which ploughman who could read, they argued, would be content to work his furrow from dawn to dusk?

In their defence, the government was ever on the lookout for seditious rumblings among the masses, and it seemed a questionable policy to wake them to their misery, and suggest a better life through education. The events of the summer of 1789 in Paris proved them right to some extent, and the year of 1793 saw a reactionary panic as fear of Jacobin insurrection flowed around the country. This short-sighted view of the moneyed classes was perhaps the greatest barrier to a national programme of education. Despite this, parishes endeavoured to keep children in their schoolrooms for as long as possible – at least to keep them occupied, as this, on the whole, was the only real value of much of Britain's education at the time. Literacy was something of an unusual skill, with three children in four unable to read, write or do basic arithmetic. However, individual philanthropists, many of them industrialists, set about trying to right the wrongs perpetrated for centuries on the poor worker.

For the most part, children went to 'dame schools', which charged a fee of two pence or three pence a week per child. There were no standards for schoolmasters, and these could range from parish curates to well-read teenagers. John Collier the satirical cartoonist and poet taught in various schools in Lancashire when he was only fourteen. There was, in some quarters, the opinion that sympathetic schoolmistresses were better equipped to instil discipline and learning on infant children than their impatient male counterparts yet still the poor schools provided little in the way of teaching skill.

Opposite:
A typical 'dame school'. The country teacher gets on with her spinning while her pupils get on with their lessons. Late eighteenth century.

Entrance of the
Juvenile Library
at 157 New Bond
Street, London,
1801.

Schools of the time held the same horrors as might be found in the works of later authors more familiar to us such as Charles Dickens or Thomas Hughes; masters could be brutal, one of the period nicknamed 'Savage Jones' and children were no less intimidated when standing before classmates. Catherine, the daughter of ex-factory worker William Hutton, was something of a prodigy in the 1780s, as was her brother with a grasp of history and Latin from a very early age, his only direct tuition apparently coming from sweeping out the schoolroom. As for Catherine, 'she never was taught to read. She went to a writing-school at nine, where her fame had gone before her; for when she first stood up with the *History of England* in her hand, Mr Baker the master said, "Now let us hear a Bishop read."' William himself had this to say of his own time: 'I now went to school to Mr Thomas Meat, of harsh memory, who often took occasion to beat my head against the wall, holding it by the hair, but never could beat any learning into it; I hated all books but those of pictures.'

The wealthier classes educated their children at home, with tutors or governesses, but those who could not afford such luxury sent their boys to boarding or day schools and academies to learn the classics, the mark of a gentleman to be learned in Latin and Greek. As important as what one wrote was how one wrote it; calligraphy was taught with a variety of implements from crow and goose quills to brass-nibbed pens.

These were the boys who went on to university and graduated to the ranks of the establishment, perhaps after undertaking an extended 'Grand Tour' of Italy or France (though this, like the universities of the day, was frequently as much an extended and debauched holiday as it was cultural education). Upper-class girls, though, were more likely to be taught 'accomplishments' – music, needlework or genealogy: subjects that would help them attract a good marriage rather than give them any broader understanding of the world.

Another difficulty faced by the working parent, with boys in particular, was a ruling that the Statute of Apprentices would not apply to trades not in existence when it was written; it had been written in 1553. This satisfied many entrepreneur industrialists who felt hampered by the restrictions of the apprenticeship system, which was in effect a form of trade unionism instituted by guilds to protect their members. Many of the new trades in the latter half of the eighteenth century exempted the factory owner from having to deal with the full apprenticeship system. Consequently many boys would now never be trained in a trade with the protective guild system – they would never rise from apprentice to journeyman and then to master.

Sons of the gentry prepare to leave for boarding school, 1790.

The fine-looking schoolhouse at Marylebone.

Concerned at the sight of children 'running wild' on Sundays in the streets of his native Gloucester, churchman Robert Raikes (1736–1811) sought both to provide children with education and prevent the social ills which its lack inevitably created. With the aid of Thomas Stock, a curate with some teaching experience, Raikes footed the bill for Gloucester's first Sunday School, convened in the home of a Mrs Meredith in July 1780. The school was intended for children of families who could not afford day school, or for those children who worked during the week. Children were taught by a number of schoolmistresses how to read and write, using the Bible for their text, and learned the catechism. Raikes himself took great interest in the children, often visiting them in their homes and awarding prizes for progress. At first only boys were taught but later girls

Robert Raikes (1736–1811), pioneer of the national Sunday School education system. From *A New History of Methodism*, edited by W. J. Townsend, H. B. Workman and George Eayrs, 1909.

attended as well. Sunday Schools in Britain already existed – one of the first established by the Wesleyan convert Hannah Bell in High Wycombe in 1769 – but Raikes was in a unique position to publicise the idea; he had inherited the *Gloucester Journal* from his father in 1757 and in 1783 wrote an anonymous letter in the paper, reporting the success of the school. John Wesley (1703–91) wrote in his diary, 'I find these schools springing up wherever I go. Perhaps God may have some deeper end therein than men are aware of. Who knows but some of them may become nurseries for Christians?' Wesley further publicised the Sunday Schools by reprinting Raikes's original letter in his *Arminian Magazine*, spreading the news of it throughout the Methodist movement. In 1788 it was reprinted again in the *Gentleman's Magazine* and enjoyed national interest. By 1795 over three-quarters of a million children attended Sunday School, taught by volunteers. Raikes had pioneered a national education system, all without government patronage. He was granted an audience with Queen Charlotte, who expressed her approval and encouraged others to follow his example.

Coming from School; colour litho by Thomas Stothard (1755–1834).

'A view of the poor house of Datchworth in Herts addressd to the overseers of England'. Image taken from *An account of the four persons found starved to death*, written by one of the jurymen on the inquisition on their bodies, 1769.

Raikes's efforts were further spread by the support of London Baptist William Fox. Fox had been keen on the idea of education but found it too daunting a task to accomplish alone. However, in 1785, with Raikes's advice, and the help of friends in the City of London, Fox endeavoured to unite both churchmen and Dissenters alike with his 'Society for the Establishment and Support for Sunday Schools'. This eventually became the 'Sunday School Union'. Raikes, Fox and others were typical of the reforming zeal which soon gripped the country.

Help for the underprivileged was handled mostly by local parishes and the poor box, as dictated by the Old Poor Law, instituted in 1601 under Queen Elizabeth I. The '43rd Elizabeth' as this law came to be called, stipulated that the people had the right to work, and recognised the responsibility of society to provide them with work. In pursuit of this obligation, parishes established shelter for their 'deserving' poor in workhouses and poorhouses (vagrants and other 'undeserving poor' were to be flogged and driven out of the parish). With the increase in industry in the eighteenth century these workhouses appeared to be a source of cheap labour. By 1776 there were nearly 2,000 workhouses across

England and Wales with over 100,000 inmates. A workhouse catered for paupers of every age, as combination overnight shelters, orphanages, nurseries for infants and nursing homes for the elderly. In 1782 the Gilbert Act streamlined the system on a county basis to offer shelter only for the aged, orphaned and infirm; this provided poor relief in the home of the able-bodied pauper without taking him or her into care. This was augmented by the 'Speenhamland system', instituted by local magistrates in Berkshire in response to the grain shortage of 1795 which caused widespread misery: it was a means-tested relief to supplement a labourer's income, which met the critical needs of the moment but proved unsatisfactory as a long-term solution, since it tended to drive down wages and left the parish to top up workers' incomes.

The pass-room at Bridewell, the clearing house where female vagrants were confined for seven days before being sent back to their own parishes; by Thomas Rowlandson and Augustus Pugin, 1808–11.

Despite the crushing poverty experienced by those who lost their traditional livelihoods, were unceremoniously ejected from employment or simply lacked the physical ability to sustain a life of hard toil, the Industrial Revolution provided a higher standard of living for many, and with this, the realisation that poverty and social neglect could be conquered as well. And thanks to an awakening conscience driven by religious movements such as the Evangelical revival, the period saw the growth of a welfare and education system still in existence today.

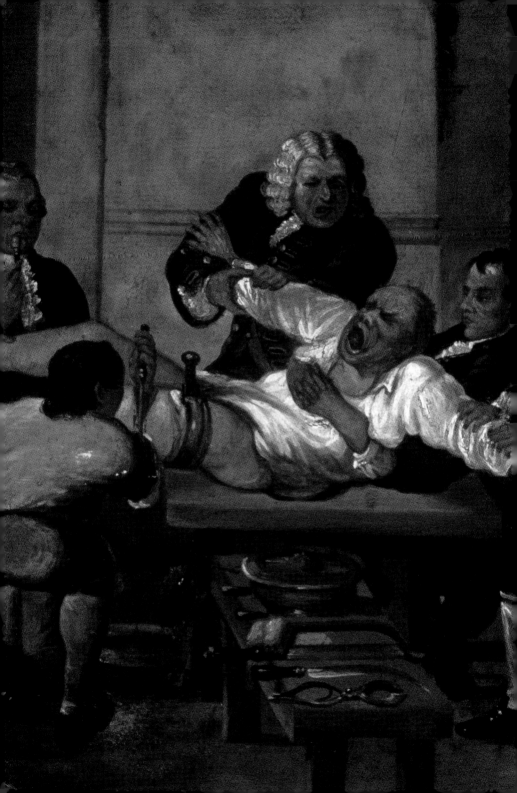

HEALTH

DESPITE the dreadful living conditions of the poor, infant mortality rates dropped in the industrialised period, even with the creation of new urban slums in the smoke-darkened mill towns of the north. There had always been a lifelong acceptance of the premature deaths of children, as historian Edward Gibbon described in 1793 when considering his own early years:

> The death of a new-born child before that of its parents may seem an unnatural, but it is strictly a probable event; since of any given number, the greater part are extinguished before their ninth year...So feeble was my constitution, so precarious my life, that in the baptism of each of my brothers, my father's prudence repeated my Christian name of Edward, that in case of the departure of the eldest son, this patronymic appellation might be still perpetuated in the family.

Medicine in the eighteenth century was becoming a technical science, the laboratory now expanding to accommodate the new social stresses created by industrialisation. Some doctors, such as Dr Aikin in Manchester, recognised how the appalling living conditions of the poor factory-worker affected the human condition, both physically and mentally. In many ways medicine of the day had a more holistic approach to the patient than its later focus on purely physical symptoms and pharmaceutical cures. In his description of Manchester in 1795, he said, 'The closeness with which the poor are crowded in offensive, dark, damp, and incommodious habitations, [is] a too fertile source of disease. The mischievous effects proceeding from this cause are so clearly stated, and the remedies so ably suggested in a paper addressed by Dr Ferriar to the Committee for the regulation of the police in Manchester.' Dr Aikin quoted from the paper:

Opposite:
The horrors of
a leg amputation,
late eighteenth
century.

Fevers are among the most usual effects; and I have often known consumptions which could be traced to this cause. Inveterate rheumatic complaints, which disable the sufferer from every kind of employment, are often produced in the same manner ... I am persuaded that mischief frequently arises, from a practice common in many back streets, of leaving the vaults of the privies open.

The streets that were thrown up to house the new workforce were left unpaved in many cases and soon carved by cartwheels into deep troughs. These then ran with mud and soon, the contents of chamber-pots flung from windows, and the overflowing sewage from inadequate drains. Occupiers of homes in Bootle Street, according to Dr Ferriar, were often rendered 'paralytic, in consequence of their situation in a blind alley, which exclude them from light and air. Consumption, distortion, and idiocy are common in such recesses.' Ferriar's report then described the dwellings:

The Royal College of Physicians. Image taken from *The Microcosm of London*. 1808–11.

The lodging homes, near the extremities of the town, produce many fevers, not only by want of cleanliness and air, but by receiving the most offensive objects into beds, which never seem to undergo any attempt towards cleaning them, from their first

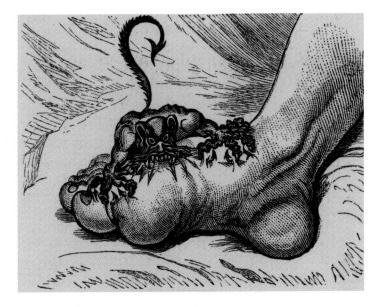

A little devil sinks his teeth into the swollen foot of a gout sufferer. Gout, a 'rich man's disease' was attributed to too much red meat, red wine and port – not the average fare at a labourer's table; engraving, 1799.

purchase till they rot under their tenants ... The horror of those houses cannot easily be described; a lodger fresh from the country often lies down in a bed filled with infection by its last tenant, or from which the corpse of a victim to fever has only been removed a few hours before.

Within the factories themselves however, a host of new ills awaited the labourer. Mutilations from uncovered machinery were common, but the greater threat was perceived to be from epidemic infection within the close confines of the factories. There was no health authority to control such matters – when infectious fever broke out in 1784 at one of the cotton mills in Manchester, residents approached magistrates who contacted local doctors. Physician Thomas Percival was asked to head up the task force. He and his colleagues had no doubt the fever stemmed from the work practices within the mills: 'supported, diffused and aggravated by the ready communication of contagion to numbers crowded together; by the accession to its virulence from putrid effluvia; and by the injury done to young persons through confinement and too long continued labour; to which several evils the cotton mills have given occasion'. Percival did not stop there, recommending 'a long recess from labour at noon, and a more early dismission from it in the evening' – this for all employees but particularly for those aged under fourteen. Dr Aikin added:

The prevalence of fever among persons employed in cotton mills might be lessened by an attention on the part of the overseers to the following circumstances, besides a due regard to ventilation. Personal cleanliness should be strongly recommended and encouraged; and the parents of children so employed, should be enjoined to wash them every morning and evening, to keep their shoes and stockings in good condition, and above all, never to send them to work early in the morning without giving them food.

The physician was on the highest rung of the medical ladder, and the surgeon considered beneath this, associated as he was with his origins as a tooth-extractor in the barbershop. A barber-surgeon performed dental operations, and the ancient therapy of blood-letting (the source of the traditional red and white barbershop pole). It became as fashionable as taking snuff to be bled by one's personal surgeon, who used specially designed instruments for the task, one such based on a spring-clasp mechanism which sliced several shallow tracks across the most appropriate limb in question.

Dr Edward Jenner vaccinates a boy against smallpox, 1796.

Smallpox was a great curse which killed one in three of those who contracted it – but the year 1796 saw the great breakthrough achieved by Dr Edward Jenner, who vaccinated a young boy against the deadly disease. Although inoculation had been introduced from India and China in the early 1700s, it was dangerous and commonly resulted in serious illness and occasionally death; it was not until Jenner's work that the safer vaccination method was used. He found that milkmaids, though often infected by cowpox brought from contact with cattle, did not usually fall victim to smallpox. It was Jenner's hypothesis that the less virulent cowpox was a safer means of improving human immunity to smallpox; his experiments proved him correct. The word 'vaccination' derives from his work, from the Latin *vacca,* for 'cow'

For the most part, unpaid medical attention was the province of the parson and some performed their duties well: 'The poor entirely confided their maladies to him,' wrote the widow of one parson-cum-village doctor, 'and he had the satisfaction of being to them eminently useful. All his drugs were got from London, a record was kept of each case of sickness and of the remedies applied...' Many Georgian medicines had splendid titles such as Daffy's Famous Elixir Salutis; there was also Dr James's Powder of antimony as a general cure-all, 'Gentle-Jog', 'Rub-a-dub' as an embrocation, and the alarming 'Dead-stop' – not to mention 'Up-with-it-then' which apparently was most useful in the bedroom. The opium-based 'laudanum' was a common but deadly and addictive painkiller combining morphine and cocaine with ethanol, and was an ingredient in many 'tonics'. Some treatments seemed almost superstitious, not dissimilar to burying a dead cat in the threshold of a house. William Hutton had the misfortune to fall gravely ill in December 1783, and recorded the details:

The village parson visits a dying parishioner, 1770.

My family was thrown into the utmost distress, by my suffering … On Sunday evening, Dec. 21, I began to feel slight pains, but was ignorant of the complaint. On Monday I took jalap, [a resinous 'cathartic' herbal tonic] and grew worse. On Tuesday a conceited apothecary was sent for, who was as unacquainted with the disorder as myself. On Wednesday Dr. Ash was called in, and told me it was an inflammation in the bowels. He also informed my friends, that there was little hope; that my blood was as thick as a jelly, and as yellow as a guinea; but added, "We must not lose him if we can help it, for he is a useful man." He saw the case desperate, and acted a bold part: bled me three times the first day, again the next, repeating it to six times. I underwent eight medical operations in one day, and was still worse. Thursday I was put into, a warm bath. Friday the same. Death was expected. I had no sleep during three days and nights. A small symptom on Saturday, at midnight, took place in my favour. The doctor visited me on Sunday at noon, and holding the curtain in his hand, said, "You are as safe as a bug in a rug."

Hospitals in the eighteenth century were run by philanthropic support. Some factory complexes were wise enough to employ a doctor's services – although doubtless born of philanthropic motives, it made business sense to keep one's workers healthy, or at least capable of performing their duties. Article 10 of the First Factory Act in 1802 stipulated that if 'any infectious Disorder appears to prevail in any Mill or Factory as aforesaid, it shall be lawful for [the

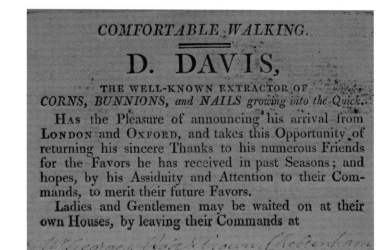

A trade card for a chiropodist offering services to the wealthy.

inspectors] to require the Master or Mistress of any such Mill or Factory to call in forthwith some Physician, or other competent medical Person' – this was done for two reason: 'for preventing the spreading of the Infection and for restoring the Health of the Sick'. Even more alarming to industry was the final blast of the statute: 'that any Expenses incurred in consequence of the Provisions aforesaid for medical Assistance, shall be discharged by the Master or Mistress of such Mill or Factory.' It was, in a way, the first step towards a free health service, whereby the worker became as much a responsibility as an investment – industrial capitalism would never be the same again.

Illustration of Nelson's funeral car; his funeral took place on 9 January 1806 amidst unprecedented scenes of public interest and emotion.

Places to Visit

NATIONAL TRUST SITES

For National Trust sites, go to the www.nationaltrust.org.uk and search for the relevant house.

Quarry Bank Mill and Styal Estate, Styal, Wilmslow, Cheshire SK9 4LA.
Water-powered cotton mill and workers' village built in 1784.

Cornish Mines and Engines, Pool, nr Redruth, Cornwall TR15 3NP.
Restored beam engines used to drain the copper and china clay mines of Cornwall, and to raise men and ore 550 feet from the mine floor.

Patterson's Spade Mill, 751 Antrim Road, Templepatrick, Co. Antrim BT39 0AP. A water-driven mill for making steel spades, active during the Industrial revolution and still operative.

Finch Foundry, Sticklepath, Okehampton, Devon EX20 2NW.
The last working water powered forge in England.

Ravenscar, Scarborough, North Yorkshire YO13 0NE
The ruins of the Ravenscar Alum Works, North Yorkshire, represent an early stage in the development of the chemical industry.

Calke Abbey, Ticknall, Derby, Derbyshire DE73 7LE.
Grand country baronial house in 600 acres.

Stainsby Mill, Hardwick Estate, Doe Lea, Chesterfield, Derbyshire S44 5QJ. A fully functioning water-powered flour mill

Horsey Windpump, Horsey, Great Yarmouth, Norfolk NR29 4EF.
Five-storey drainage windpump.

Dunster Working Watermill, Mill Lane, Dunster, nr Minehead, Somerset TA24 6SW. There has been a mill on this site since Domesday; the current one dates from the eighteenth century.

Shugborough Estate, Milford, nr Stafford, Staffordshire ST17 0XB.
Rare survival of a complete mid-eighteenth century estate, with all major buildings including mansion house, servants' quarters, model farm and walled garden.

Gray's Printing Press, 49 Main Street, Strabane, Co. Tyrone BT82 8AU.
Eighteenth-century provincial printing press behind an old shop front.

Branscombe, Seaton, Devon EX12 3DB.
Working thatched forge and associated bakery and mill.

Gibson Mill, Hardcastle Crags Hollin Hall, Crimsworth Dean, Hebden Bridge, West Yorkshire HX7 7AP.
Environmental project housed within the old mill, built 1800.

OTHER SITES

Cromford Mill Mill Rd., Matlock, Derbyshire DE4 3RQ.
Website: www.arkwrightsociety.org.uk/cromford
The world's first successful water powered cotton spinning mill, complete factory system.

Masson Mills, Derby Road, Matlock, Derbyshire.
Masson Mills at Matlock Bath (1783) are the finest surviving examples of Arkwright's cotton mills.

Cromford, Derbyshire, is a substantial village constructed by Arkwright to house his employees at the nearby Cromford Mill.

New Lanark, South Lanarkshire, Scotland ML11 9DB,
Website: www.newlanark.org
Robert Owen's restored cotton mill and associated village with working steam engine.

James Watt Ephemera, Hunterian Museum, University of Glasgow, University Avenue, G12 8QQ. Website: www.hunterian.gla.ac.uk
Statue and objects associated with the engineer who powered the Industrial Revolution.

Portsmouth historic dockyard. Website: www.historicdockyard.co.uk
Eighteenth-century dockyard, HMS Victory and Nelsonian museum celebrates the Royal Navy at the turn of the nineteenth century.

Helmshore Mills Textile Museum, Holcombe Road, Helmshore, Rossendale, BB4 4NP. Website: www.lancashire.gov.uk/museums
Eighteenth-century water-powered fulling mill.

Ironbridge Gorge Museum, Coalbrookdale, Telford, TF8 7DQ.
Website: www.ironbridge.org.uk
The original site of the Industrial Revolution, with ten museums.

National Waterways Museum, Stoke Bruerne, Nr Towcester, NN12 7SE.
Website: www.nwm.org.uk
The history of Britain's canal network.

Cambridge Museum of Technology, The Old Pumping Station, Cheddars Lane, Cambridge, CB5 8LD. Website: www.museumoftechnology.com
Part of the Industrious East group of museums, industrial heritage sites and farms.

Gressenhall Farm & Workhouse, Gressenhall, Dereham, Norfolk NR20 4DR.
Website: ww.museums.norfolk.gov.uk
Workhouse built in 1777, providing tours and exhibits of life both in the workhouse and the adjoining farmstead.

The Trevithick Trail, Penydarren, Merthyr Tydfil, to Abercynon.
Website: www.trevithicktrail.co.uk
Britain's first 'railway', operated by a prototype steam locomotive built by Richard Trevithick in 1804.

INDEX

Page numbers in italic refer to illustrations